ART NOUVEAU
&
EARLY ART DECO
TYPE & DESIGN

ART NOUVEAU & EARLY ART DECO TYPE & DESIGN

FROM THE ROMAN SCHERER CATALOGUE
EDITED BY THEODORE MENTEN

DOVER PUBLICATIONS, INC.
NEW YORK

Published in Canada by General Publishing Company, Ltd.,
30 Lesmill Road, Don Mills, Toronto, Ontario.
Published in the United Kingdom by Constable and Company, Ltd., 10 Orange Street, London WC 2.

Art Nouveau and Early Art Deco Type and Design, first published by Dover Publications, Inc., in 1972, is a new selection
of pages from the catalogue (n.d.; accompanying price list
dated 1908) of Roman Scherer, a manufacturer of wood type
in Lucerne, Switzerland.

DOVER *Pictorial Archive* SERIES

International Standard Book Number: 0-486-22825-8
Library of Congress Catalog Card Number: 75-189434

Manufactured in the United States of America
Dover Publications, Inc.
180 Varick Street
New York, N.Y. 10014

ART NOUVEAU & EARLY ART DECO TYPE & DESIGN

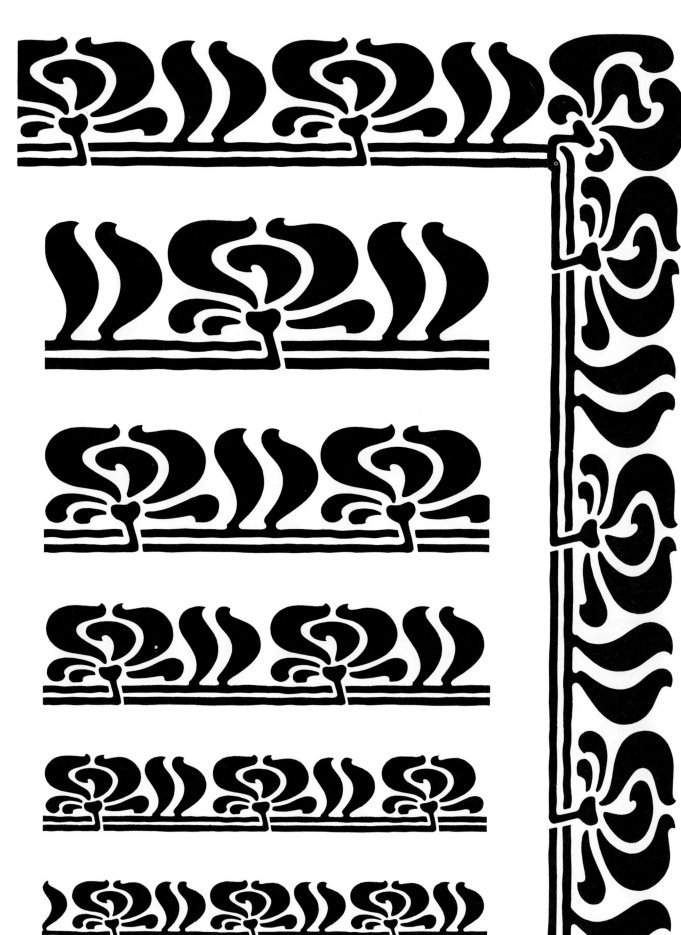

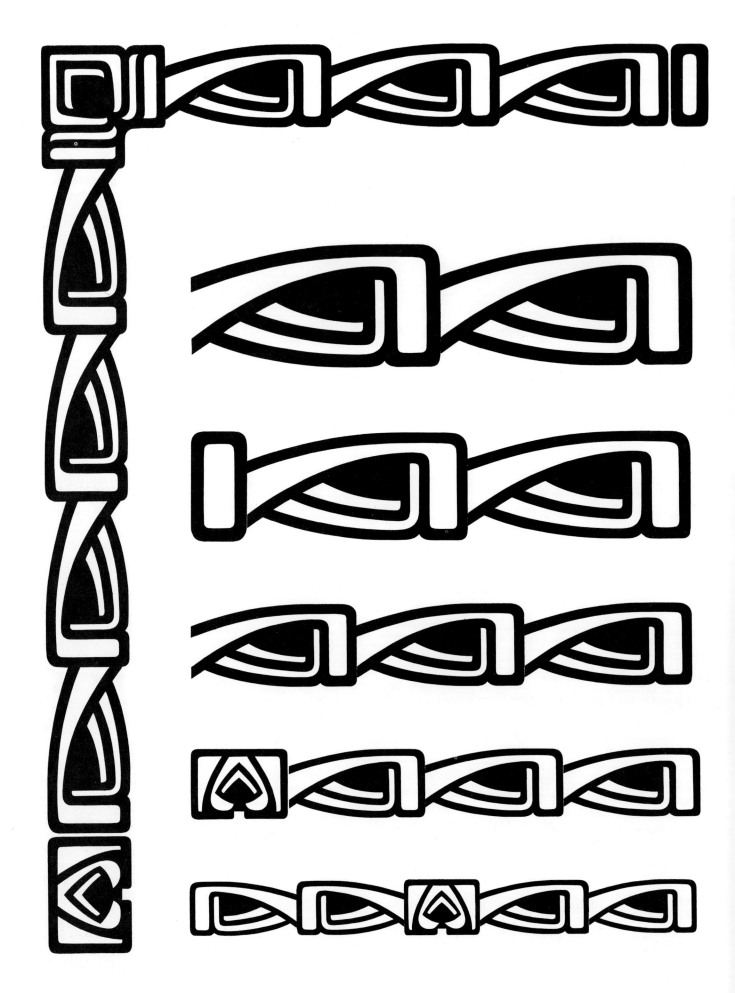

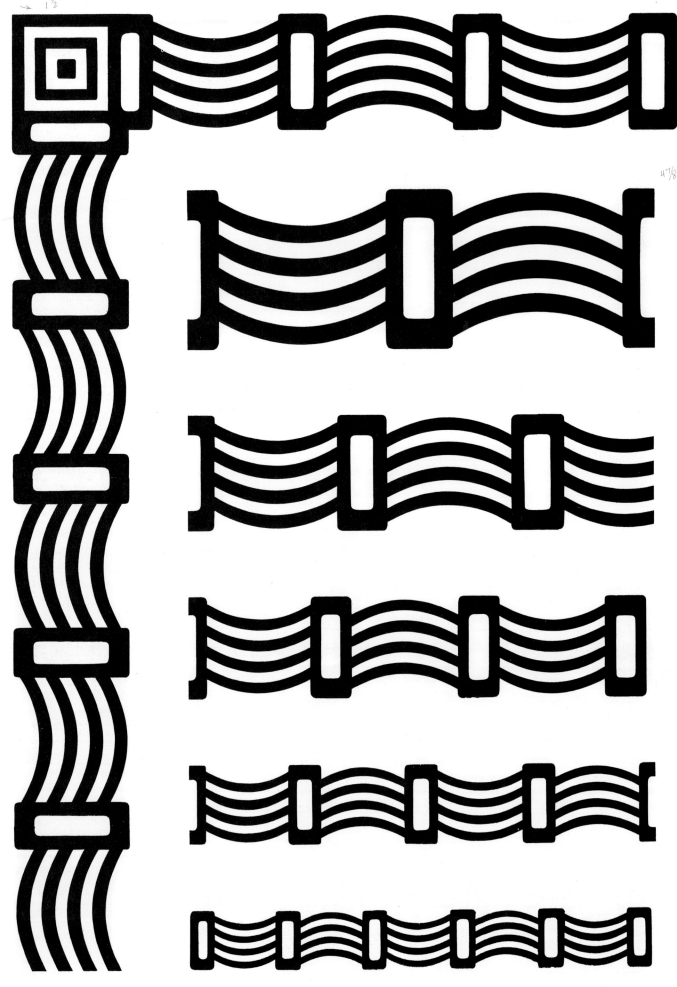

4

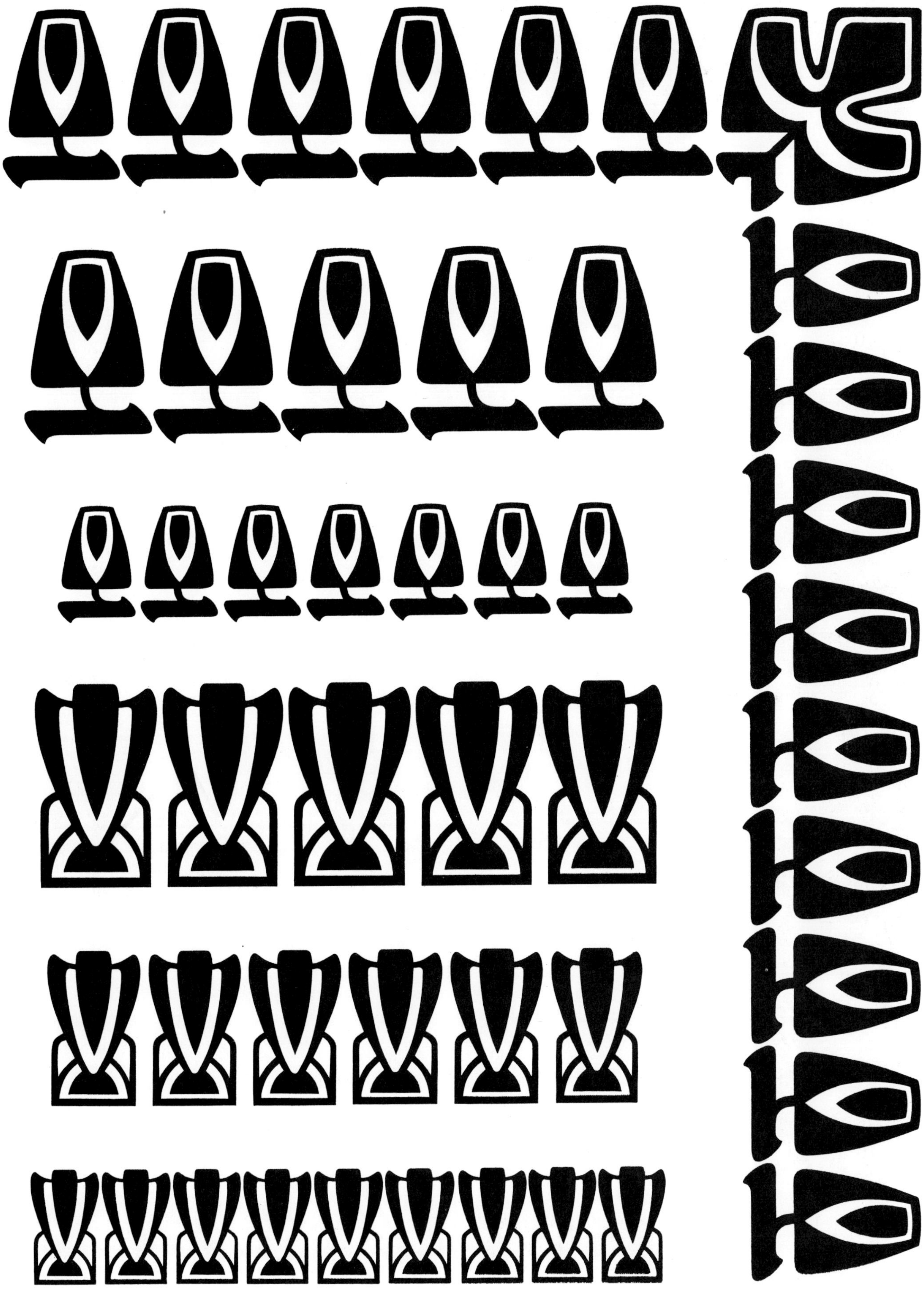

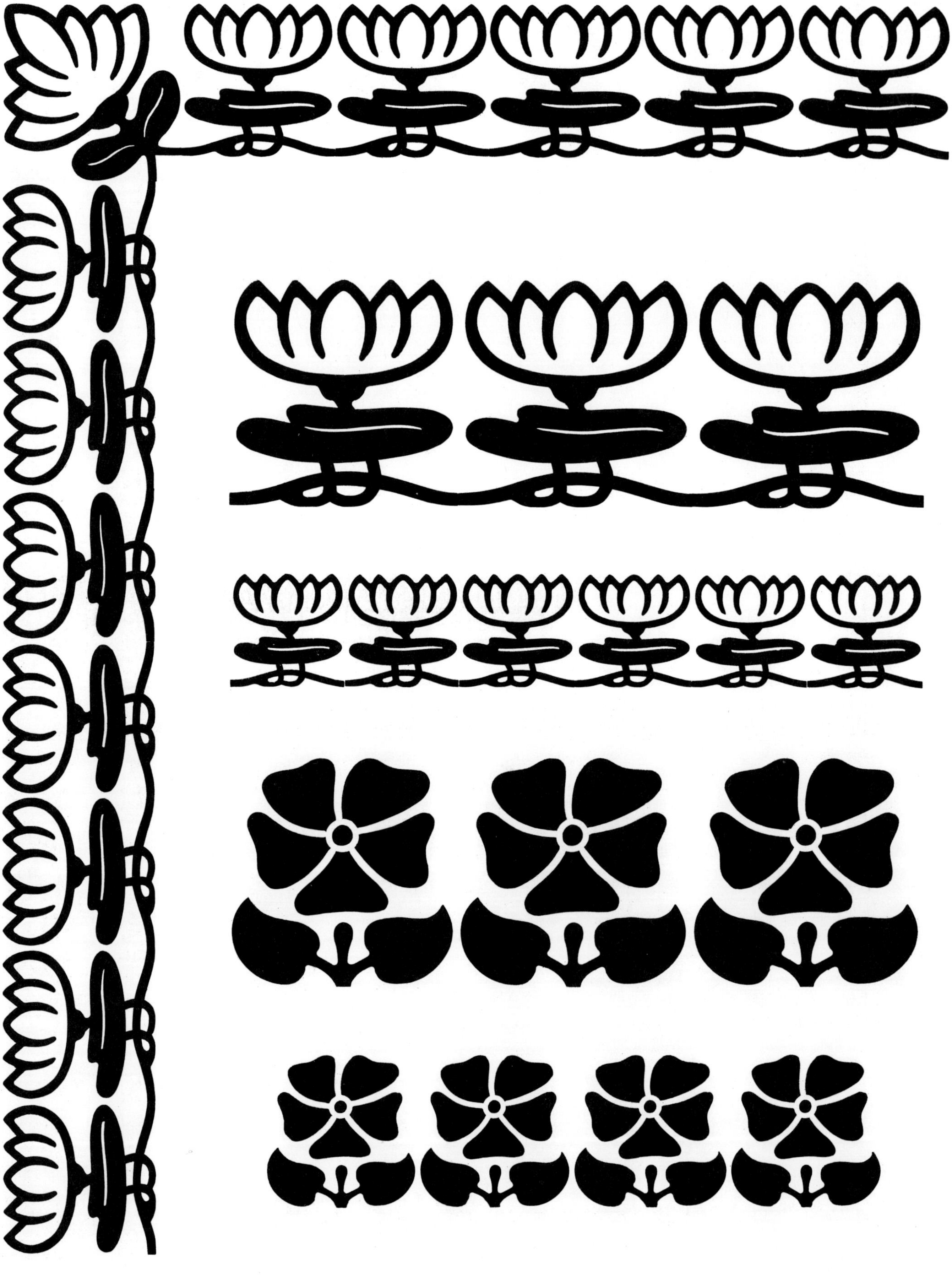

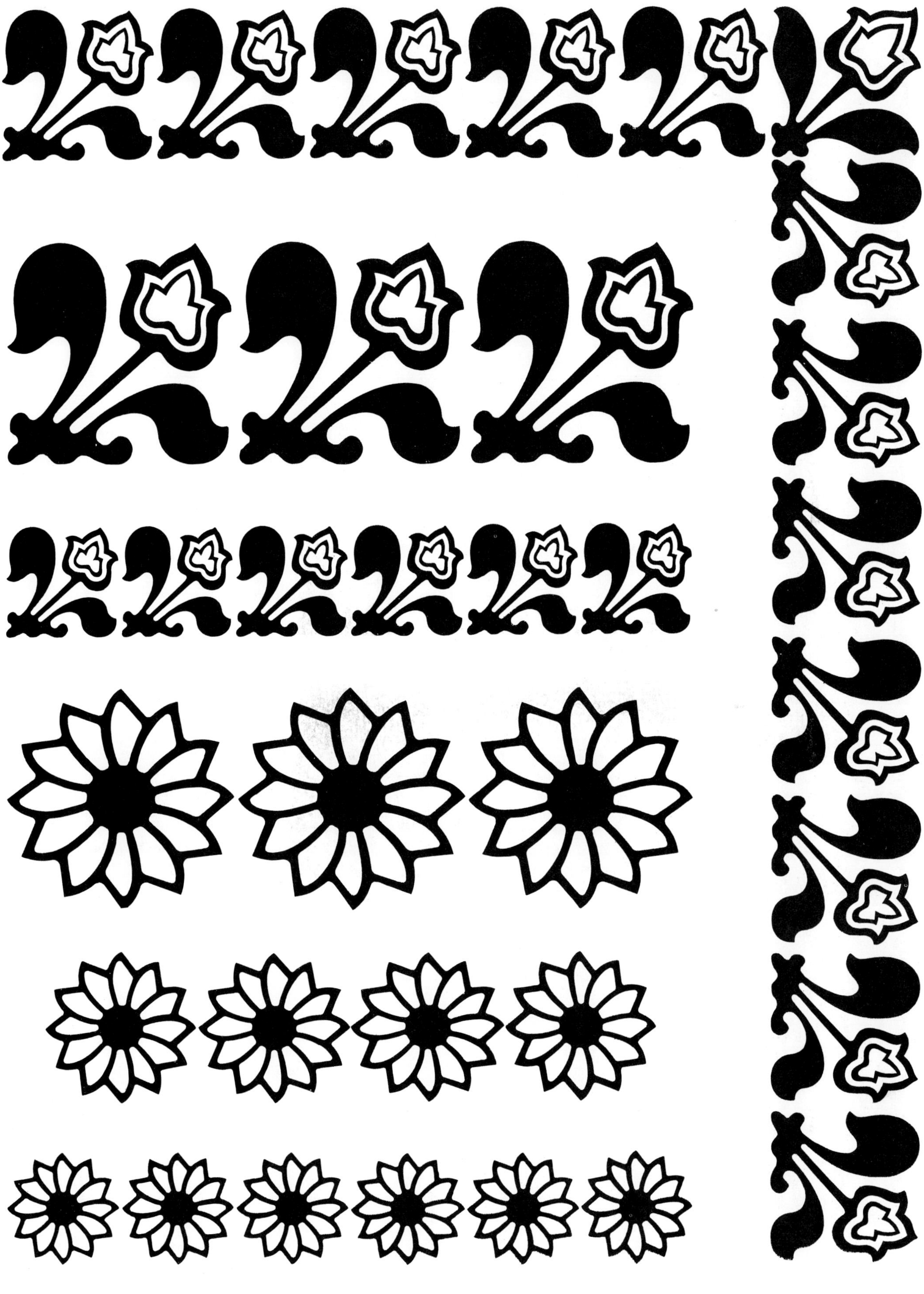

11

13

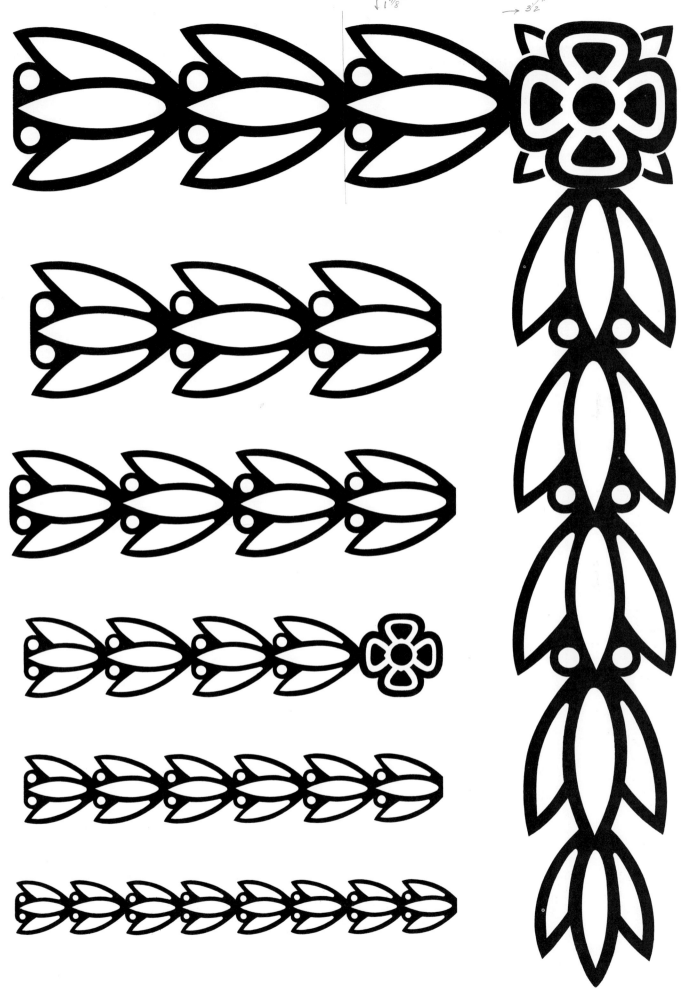

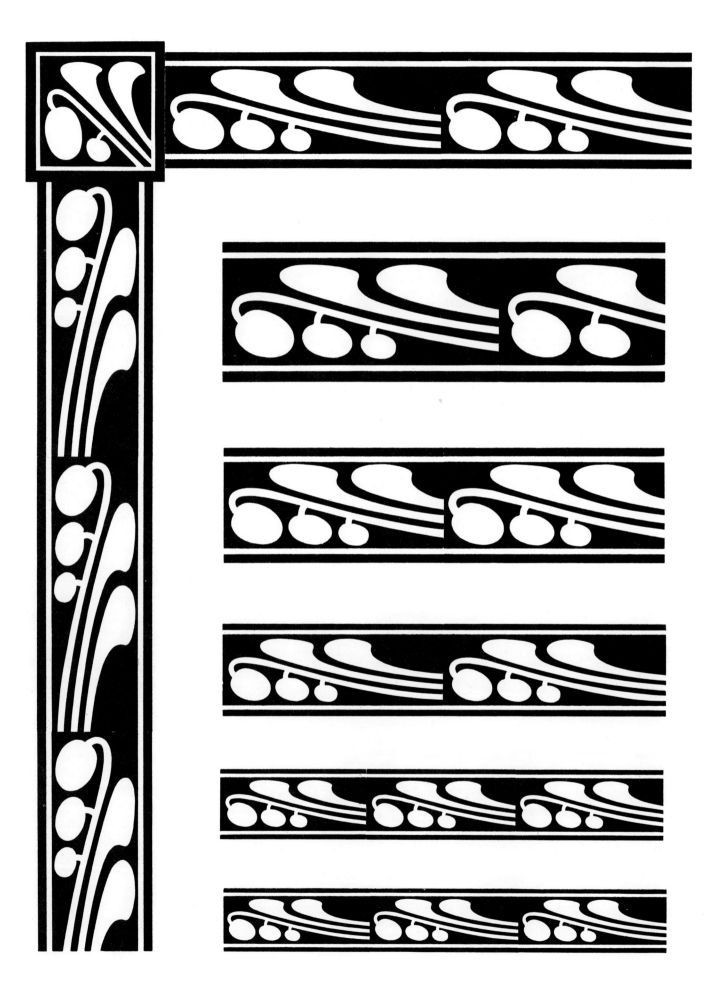

21

25

27

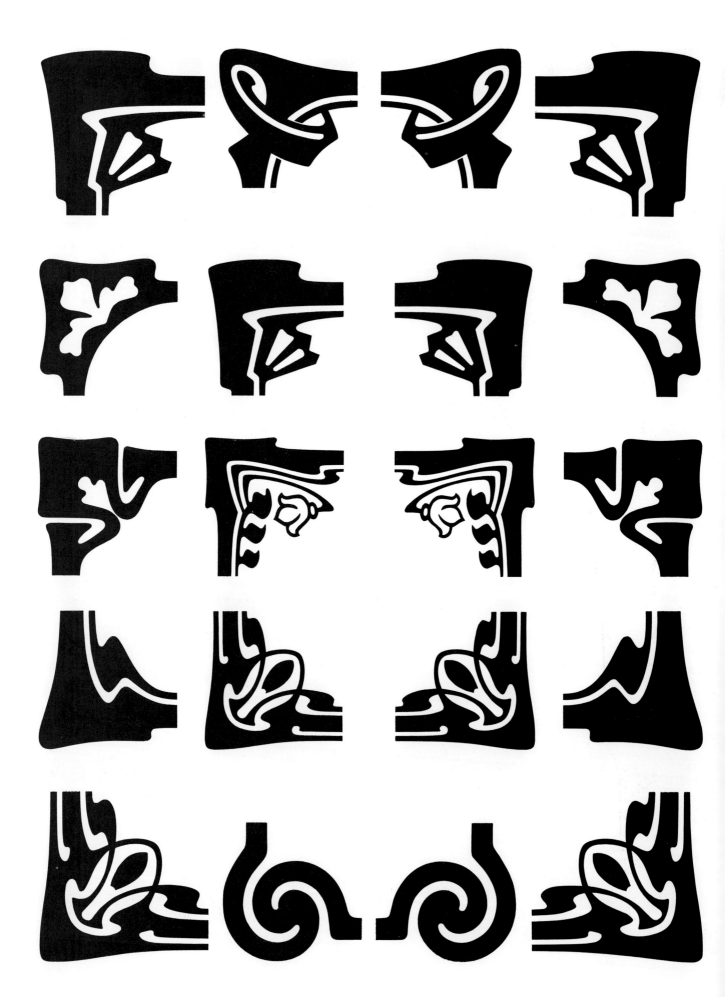

28

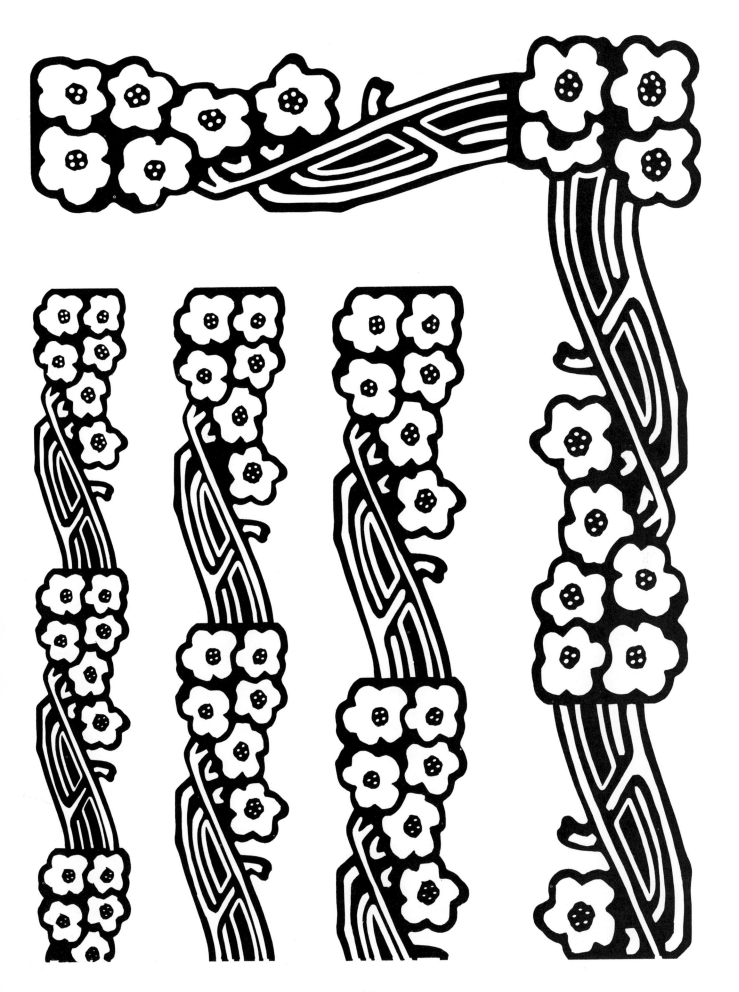

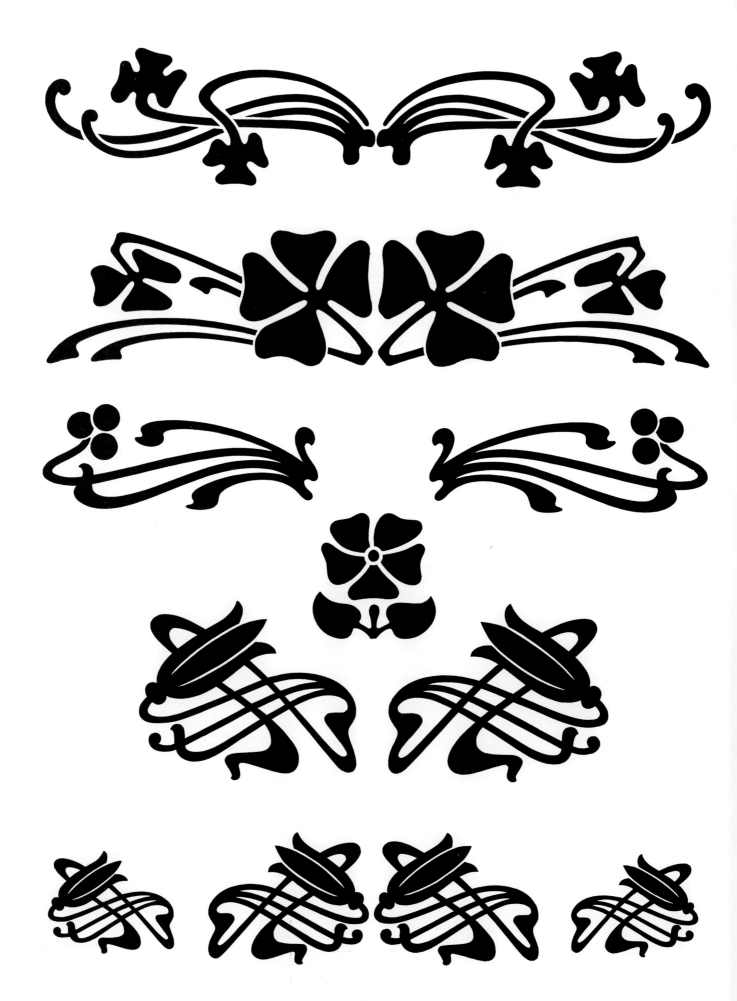

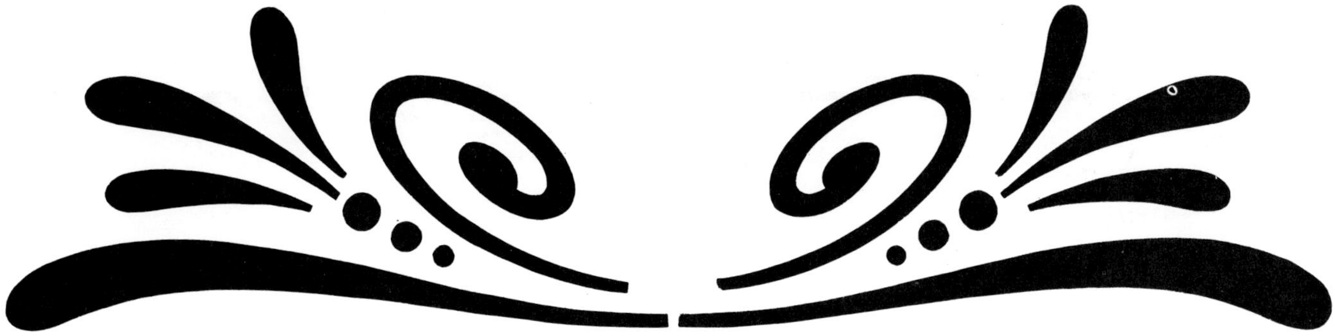

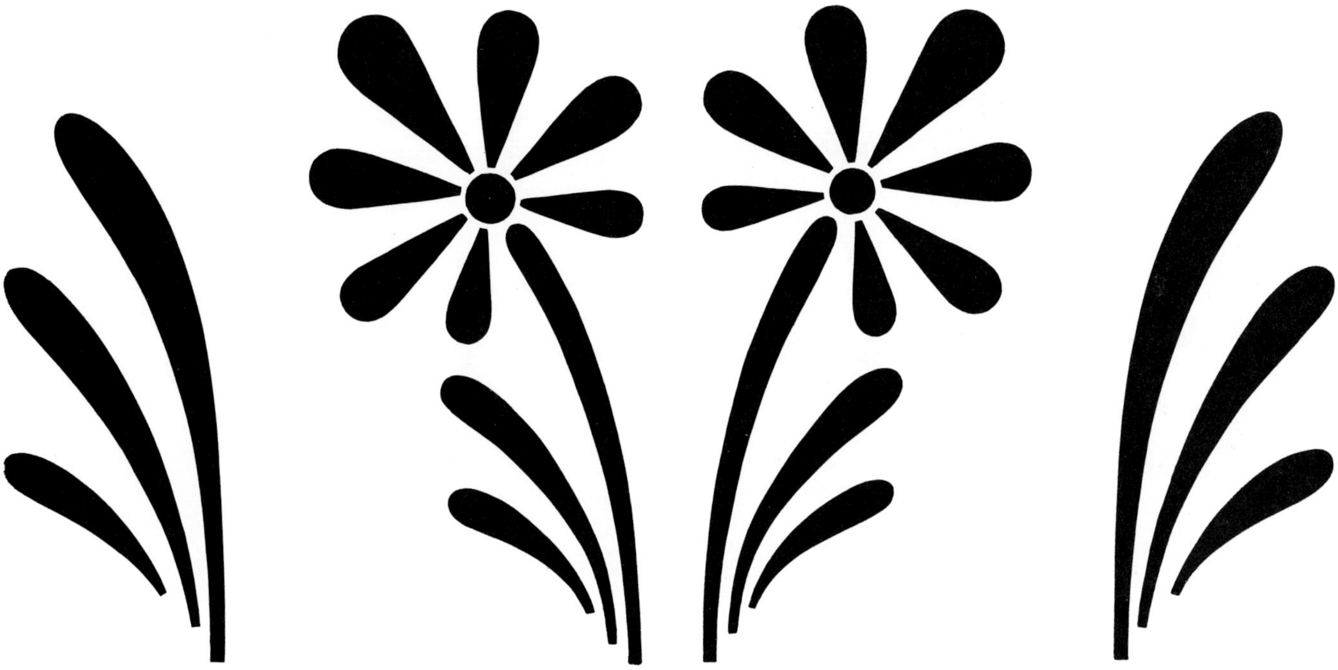

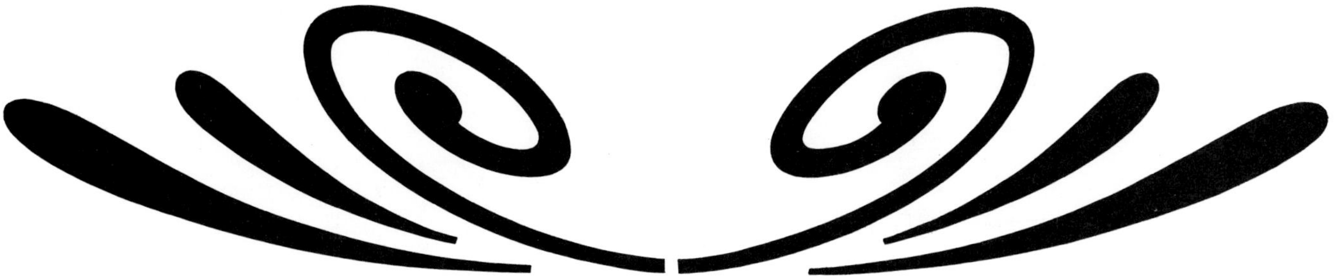

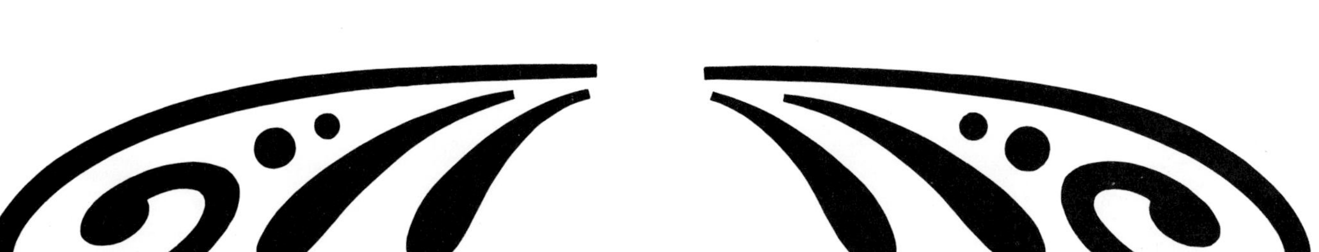

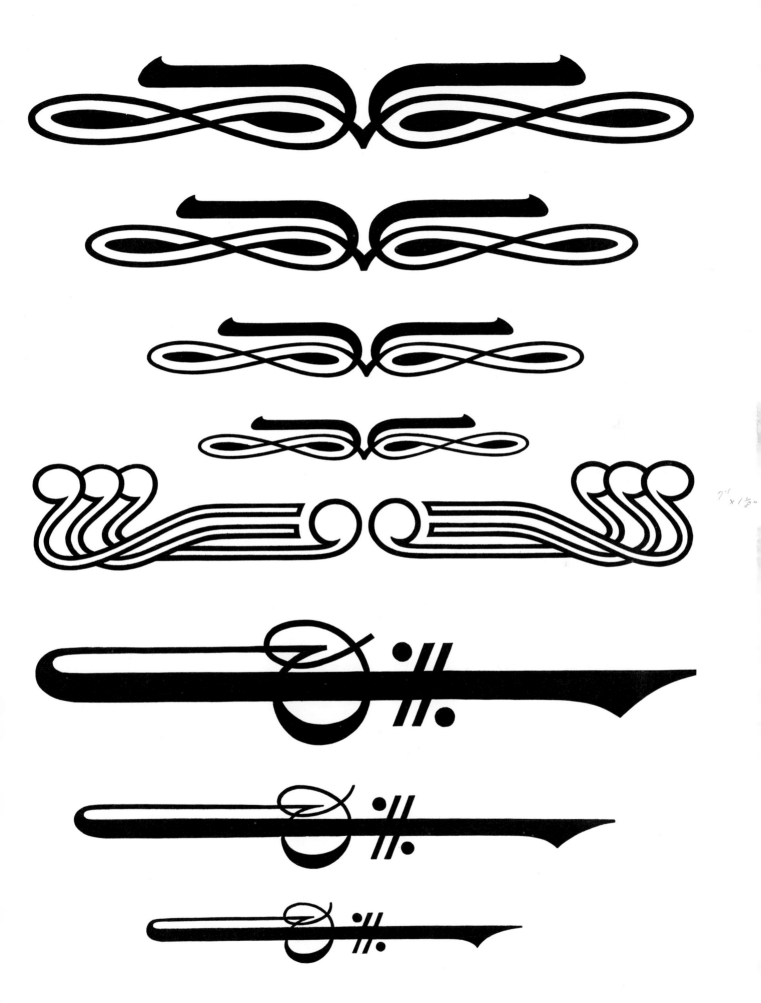

7" x 1⅛"

39

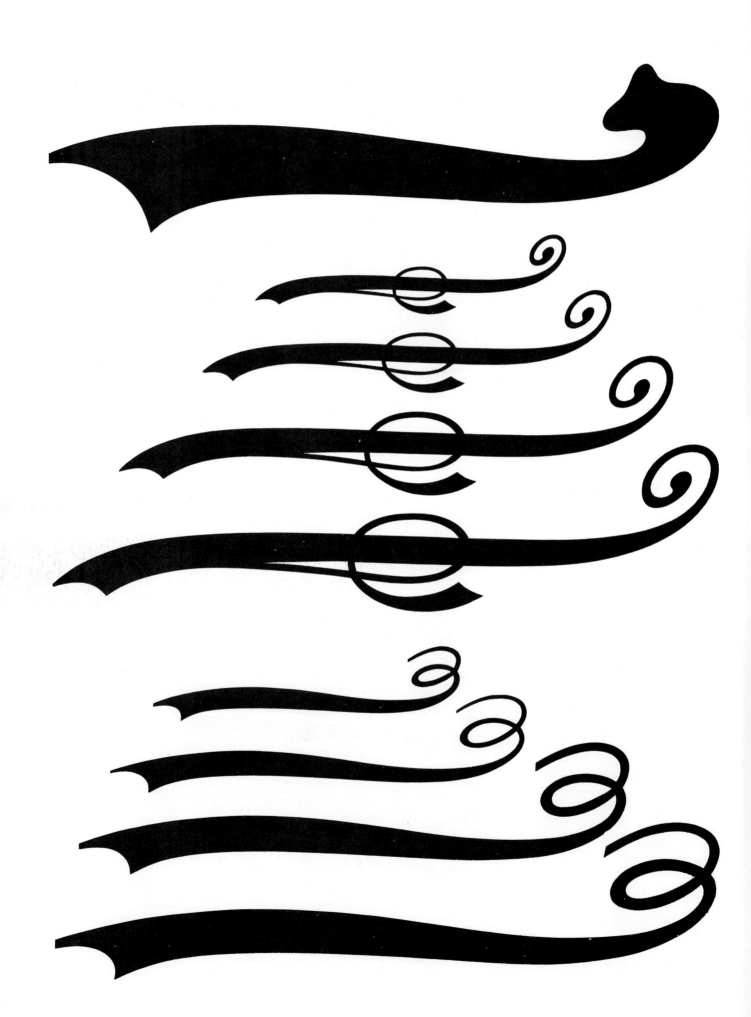

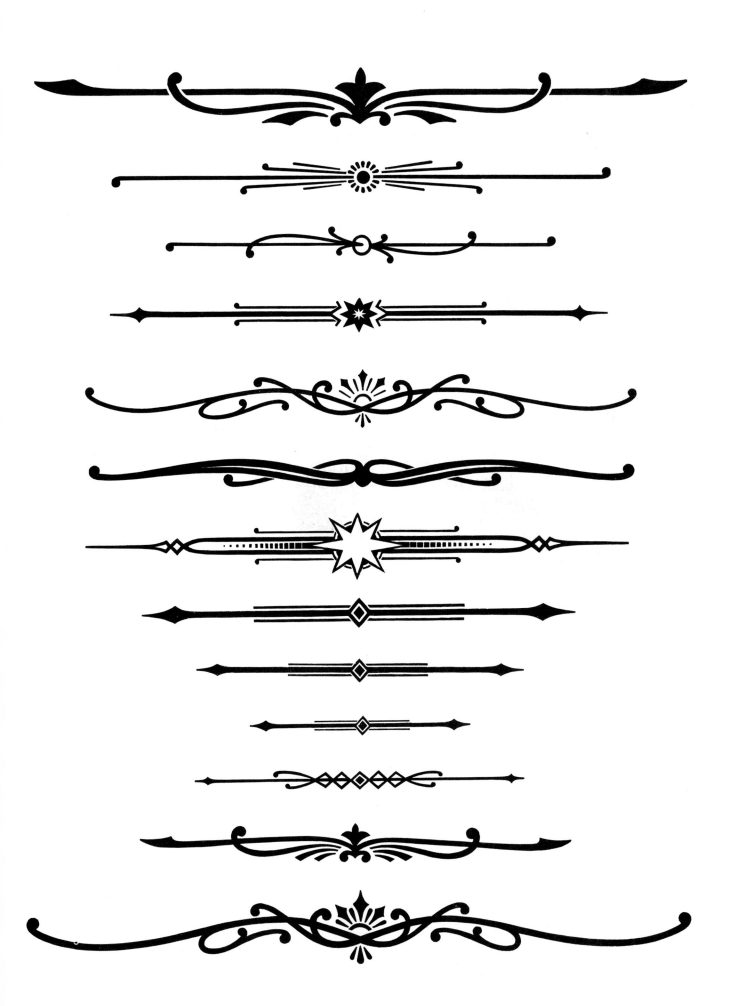

43

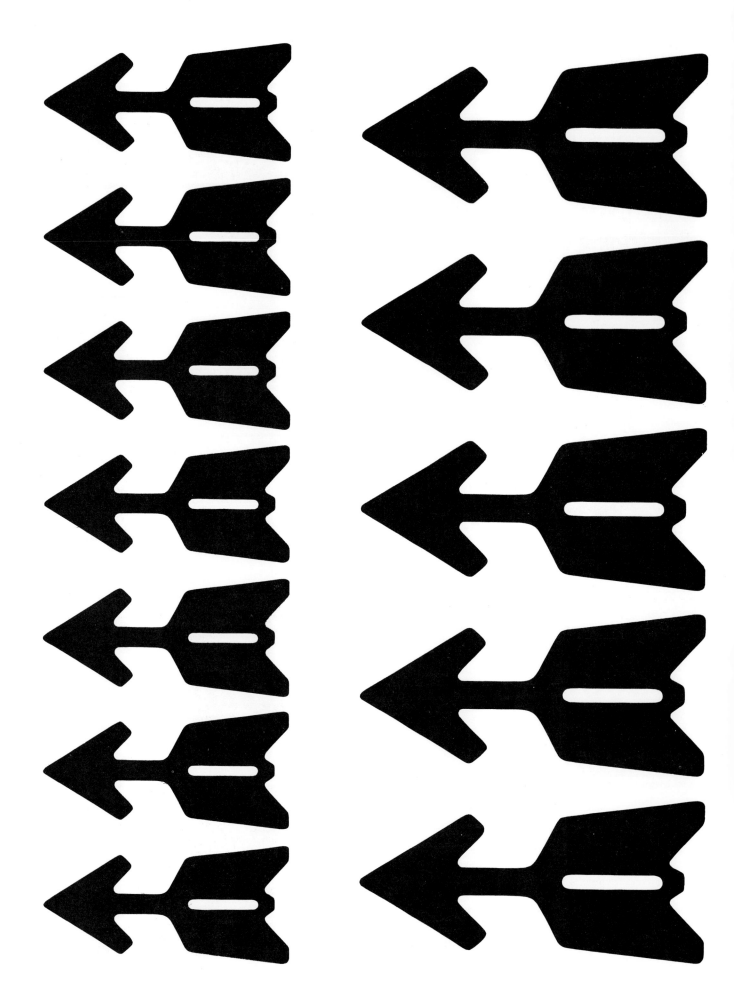

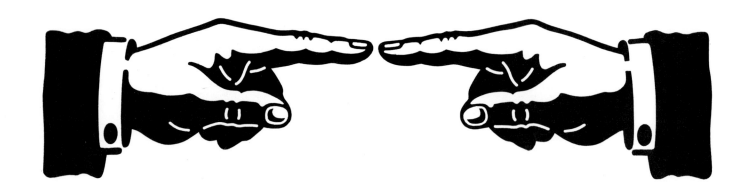

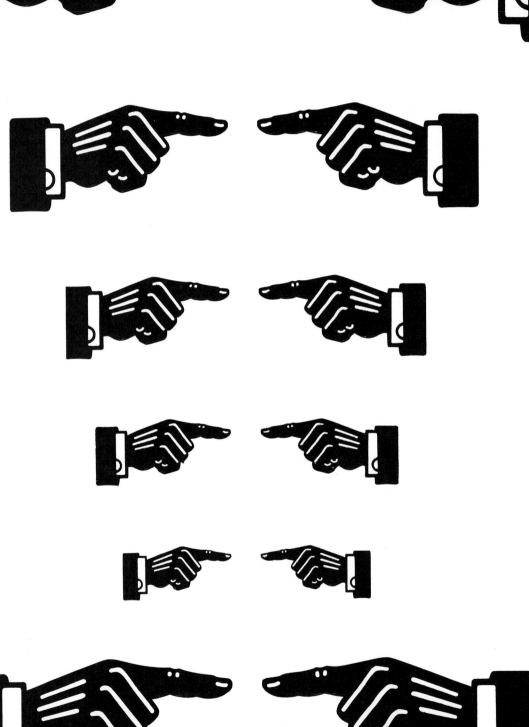

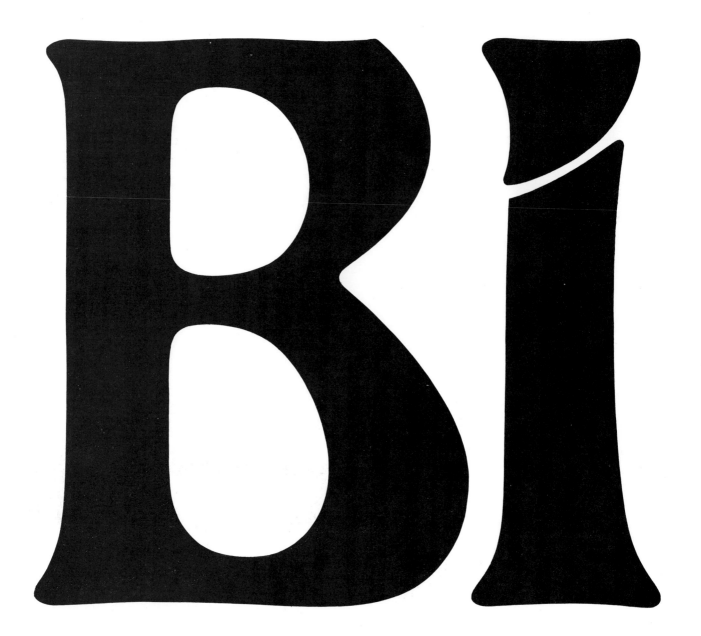

R

ROI

Bunt

RONE

Fonda

Roba 4

Ad

Kad

R

DER

Kot

Ruba

Bud

Aosta

LUZERN

Radeso 35

HAMBOURG

BRONA

Roveredo

Frankfurt

NEUENBERG

Rostock Brenda

LUZERN 35 ROME

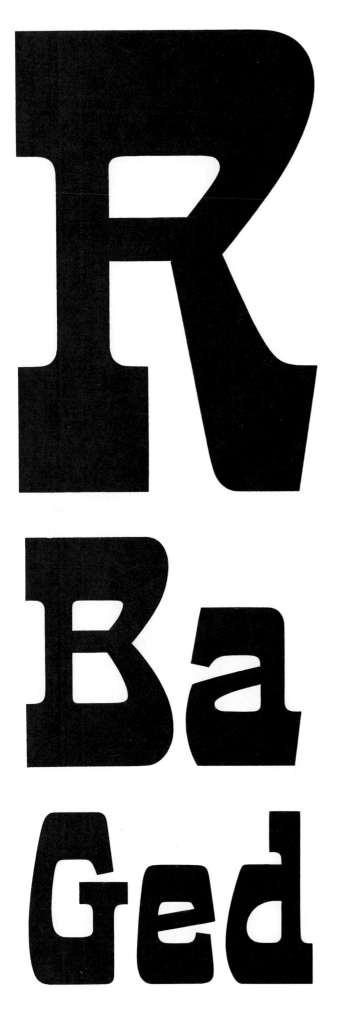

RIK

Bent

Aosta

KASAN

Nantes 3

BRAGANZA

BI

RODI

Baden

Red

Genova

AVIGNON

Koba

Granada 90

NORDHAUSEN

RI

RION

RI

Baden

Hid

Morges

Carouge

REINECK 32

RI

Ked

ROME

Nancy

Moskau

Ragusa 65

NORDHAUSEN

BIE
RONDA

RI
Bed
Dake

BERN
Davos
Ancona
Bukarest
Borkum 45
NORDERNEY

ODESSA

Karlsbad

Nordhusen

Cherbourg Brest

Madrid Barcelona

BURGES 80 LUCERNE

BADEN

Konstanz

Rustschuk

✿ LUZERN ✿

Vierwaldstättersee

GERSAU 534 WEGGIS

RIA

Luzern

BI

Kad

Reich

BENO

Rocha

Ostende

LUCERNE

Granada 23

BRANDEBURG

B

Got

Bant

WEN

Ruda

Padua

Dresden

HARBURG

Luzern 23

RI

Keid

Bruck

BERN

Nantes

LUZERN

Dresden

Posen 35

BE

Ked

RINEO

Krakau

Bukarest

Gerona 30

BRANDENBURG

Ri

Bel

Beat

Aosta

Danzig

Ronda 32

Neuenkirch

Na

Bed

Baden

Krakau

Narbonne

Bregenz 34

San Sebastian

ROBES

Neustadt

Petersburg

Kronstadt 43

Ostende Hannover

Bed
Nat
Rond

Nantes
Rostock
Bordeaux
Kronstadt
Rochefort 53
Moskau Berlin

Dresden

Grandson

Kopenhagen

Brandenburg

Nordhausen 34

Rotenburg Bregenz

Siegfried

Börsenblatt

Die Rundschau

Moskau Wien 3

Bukarest Konstanz

KIEN

ROND

LUCERNE

ROME

Padua

Ostende

LUCERNE

Nordhausen 3

Gratz Düsseldorf

KAIRO

Dresden

Grandson

Nardonnes 53

KOBURG DESSAU

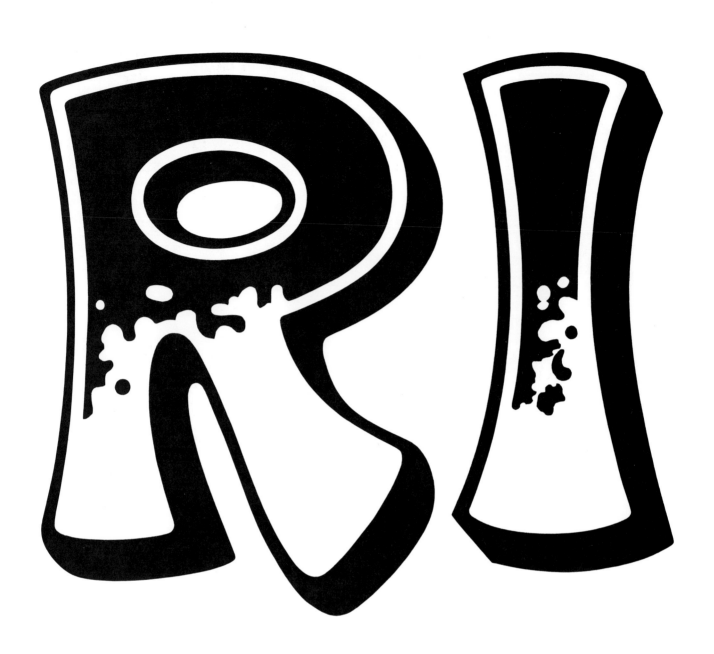

RONE

HERO

AOSTA

LUCERNE

R

K

I

ME

RED

NICE

ROMA

VARESE